How Cancer Save

Getting Through

John D Edwards

This edition published in the UK 2007
by BolamRose,
Fleet House, 8–12 New Bridge Street,
London EC4V 6AL

1 3 5 7 9 10 8 6 4 2

Designed and typeset by
Jerry Goldie Graphic Design.

Printed and bound in China Through
Sino Publishing House Ltd.

British Library Cataloguing-in-
Publication data available

ISBN-978-09555615-0-4

johndedwards.co.uk

Contents

John D Edwards, (I think John uses the D because there was already a painter called John Edwards), joined the staff at Waddington Galleries at about the same time that I was taken on at the Gallery.

I knew John painted and if I recall correctly, he showed me photographs of his work, which I liked very much. Although they were by no means "Naïve" they fitted into a loose category which also included "Art Brut" but they were sophisticated- and very funny, peopled with strange little human beings, animals and birds. John and I became friends and I continued to enjoy his work.

Then John decided to leave the gallery and move to the country. Some time later I heard he "wasn't very well", what does that mean? You hear news like that and you get on with your own life. It's difficult to comprehend what another person is living through.

It was only recently, when I was doing some work at the amazing AB Fine Art Foundry, where John now lives in his studio overlooking The Yard (filled when I first went there with an enormous Barry Flanagan Hare Sculpture) that I met John again. I began to realise how ill John had been.

John has lived through and survived his cancer, his separation from his wife and the death of his mother. This Book records with John's sensitive comments, these events. They are courageous paintings but also full of humour and wit, I laughed out aloud at "The Texan Art Dealer"

This is an uplifting record of an unbelievably difficult time for John, told with great humour.

"LIVING WELL IS THE BEST REVENGE"

Sir Peter Blake RA, London May 2007.

John in his studio in Poplar

Cruising the Neighbourhood

After several years of The Country Life I had returned to my studio in Poplar, East London. My work for a few years had been about the countryside, now I was back in the city. I felt very comfortable being back in the urban landscape that I had grown up in.

When moving house you get this snapshot of a life as a collection of possessions. Amongst my books were some old cartoon annuals. I loved these comic versions of urban life as a child and still do. I painted very quickly a series of "cartoon time" images as a celebration of being back where I belonged. Although apparently it was a fun time I did notice this big beast of a bull dog coming round the wall at me.

There was trouble in the neighbourhood.

CRUISING THE NEIGHBOURHOOD

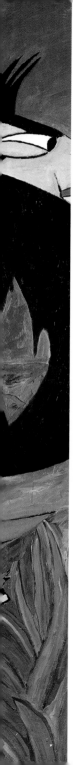

The Wolf

As I painted the big Wolf painting I was beginning to sense
something was wrong and I could see I was facing a challenge. I
felt weak but the painting was coming on strong. I was
exhausted by this painting but this powerful image was such a
potent expression of the spirit.

I've always kept this painting and had it hanging near my front
door to see off all the demons.

THE WOLF

Out of this World

At the end of 1996 I began a couple of years of treatment for cancer. Although at times working was difficult I always thought about and continued to paint. I found this not only therapeutic and sustaining but also an insight into my condition. One of my old themes "the cowboy" returned which I found reassuring but not so much a number of ghostly bride images, obviously dealing with my failed marriage of a few years before. These transformed into a series of angel paintings inspired by the discovery that I had become a host to cancer. Dark days.

As I pulled through I painted a series of hospital paintings; with my "birds" creeping in as doctors and the patients and angels as nurses.

I knew this was a good sign.

"Out of this World" is about that detached feeling that comes after the numerous operations and different therapies; the feeling of going in and out of the anaesthetic but you are still there, somewhere, waiting to return. Although these are serious matters I like the sense of playfulness which to me was an inspiration and encouragement that I would be O.K.

OUT OF THIS WORLD

Isolation

One of the reflective ghostly bride series I painted when I was
back in London. It was a sad fact that a number of white faceless
brides had begun to appear in barren landscapes way back when
I was first married and living on the farm in Gloucestershire.
They say you can learn a lot from someone's handwriting; with
me it's all there in the work, right in front of you in glorious
Technicolor.

ISOLATION

Some of the things I used to do

A few years before the cancer was diagnosed, after my marriage broke up, I hit a real low. I had "my lost weekend" (which had probably started years rather than days before). I made a decision to change my ways and several years later as I was getting well it was a pleasure to be able to look back and paint about the old days.

SOME OF THE THINGS I USED TO DO

Friends

In a waiting room I'd seen these fish and I thought 'what a simple life'. The thing about them only having a short memory of seconds I saw as a great freedom and I tried to apply this in getting through my illness, not being weighed down by the events of previous days, in fact just living in the moment. They were my friends. I wanted to put them in a painting so I placed them on my chest of drawers that stands at the end of my bed. I like the glowing qualities of the Indian yellow against the turquoise blue in this painting.

FRIENDS

Angel at Sunrise

The one time I really wept was when after a few months of exploratory operations and tests I was given a definitive diagnosis. It was cancer with a primary source and secondarys that were spreading fast.

After the months of uncertainty my tears were out of relief and for healing. This is when the angels started to appear. I now knew what I was dealing with and there were a number of options being considered. Even though this is rather a bleak and ragged angel I did feel that the sun was rising not setting.

ANGEL AT SUNRISE

Serenity (Angel Sunbathing)

I was very tired; I'd had several operations and was now having daily interferon injections. The angels were looking over me.

My body was wounded but my spirit was strong.

The angel here is gently resting as the dawn breaks. Although this is a dark painting I could see the quiet serenity of the angel, lying there being warmed by the sun.

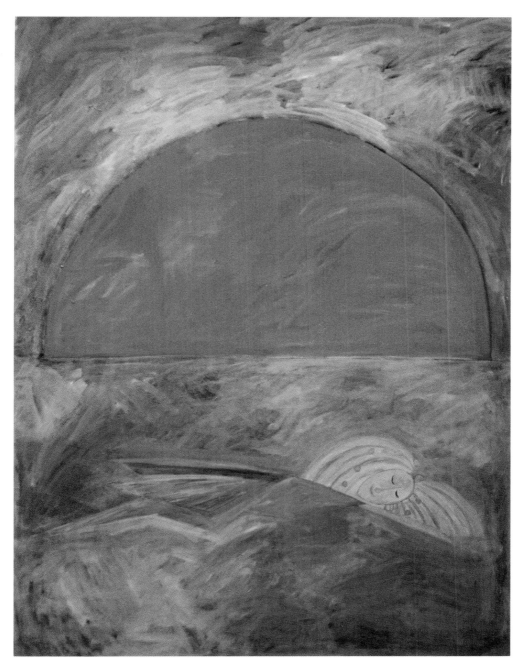

SERENITY (ANGEL SUNBATHING)

Angel of Eternal Light

It was a revelation to myself that I could live with cancer peacefully. I discovered hope and faith where I thought there would be fear.

ANGEL OF ETERNAL LIGHT

There are Angels

I realised that in fact the angels came in the form of all those caring for me. And the nurses really are angels.

THERE ARE ANGELS

Angels at Tea Time

A nice cup of tea and all that attention and warmth from the nurses, you can't beat that combination!

ANGELS AT TEA TIME

The Consultants

One day when the doctors were all around my bed, examining me in that chickenlike, startledlook way. I saw them as birds. I was heavily drugged but well aware of their intentions.

THE CONSULTANTS

The Angels Who Care for Me

I really had to dig deep at this stage in deciding the right way to go. Those wonderful nurses, those angels, helped me to have the courage to take responsibility for my own body and treatment. Another dark moment.

THE ANGELS WHO CARE FOR ME

The Sun Shines Through

Having made a crucial decision, I could see there would always be sunshine here and beyond; as long as I was true to myself.

THE SUN SHINES THROUGH

Beach Day

I found it very helpful to while away the days thinking of "the good times". I got great comfort from remembering those family holidays on the South Coast. Playing on the beach feeling you had "all the time in the world", one of Mum's magic phrases.

One weekend I told everyone I was going away whilst I stayed in my studio and peacefully painted this painting. It was like sending a postcard home saying I was doing O.K.

BEACH DAY

Dark Days

The chemotherapy was tough but I always felt it was something I should do. I never lost hope and I tried in this painting to express that feeling of "terrible beauty", as the poet W. B. Yeates put it. The human spirit is capable of overcoming so much. I like the way the little bird looks over me, another little angel.

DARK DAYS

Tree of Hopes and Dreams (Festive Angel)

The combination of chemo and radiotherapy treatments had removed me from the usual franticness of Christmas. There was a tree in the ward like a glowing fire. I sat for hours staring into its honeycombed, illuminated interior. I imagined I was free to wander in its dreamlike coloured landscape.

I had decided to embrace the treatment, so I was going to lie back and "enjoy it".

There was a golden angel on the top, poised as if about to fly. Another little sign of hope.

TREE OF HOPES AND DREAMS (FESTIVE ANGEL)

Texan Art Dealer (Cowboy)

One of my old themes which I've always found reassuring. You can do with a bit of the cowboy spirit as well as the warmth of the big sun behind you.

The cowboys, trains, birds, boats and cats, bunches of flowers, mothers and children all first appeared in a sketch book, that I still have, from when I was 5 years old.

When this image resurfaced during my illness I felt it was a great sign of hope.

The Texan Art Dealer, (Cowboy) is a portrait of the gallery dealer, a loveable rogue, who exhibited my work in Houston Texas a few years later.

COWBOY

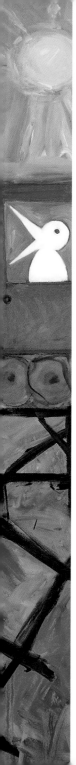

Tourist Class

In the wards and various clinic waiting rooms I got to know many of my fellow sufferers. It was like we were all travelling together, discussing our situations but not really knowing of our individual destinations. As we shared our experiences there was always reassurance and support. I had never been shown such bravery, acceptance and love.

How ever dark the journey sometimes was I never lost sight of the sunshine.

TOURIST CLASS

Pink Shoes

I really did have an active love life throughout the illness. "Pink Shoes" is a tribute to this extraordinary fact.

PINK SHOES

All Will Be Well

Thankfully there are always those vital moments of hilarity. We had just been told that we wouldn't be having radiotherapy treatment on Christmas Day or Boxing Day as they were Public (Bank) Holidays.

ALL WILL BE WELL!

Getting Through

It is a happy painting about overcoming illness, the resilience of the human spirit. This painting is a celebration. The birds, I think, represent all the consultants, doctors, angels as nurses, herbalists, faith healers, family, friends, priests, witches, nuns, massage practitioners vicars and everyone who looked after me. I am really beginning to simplify my palette here. I wanted to paint a yellow painting like the sunshine.

GETTING THROUGH

After Visiting (Easter Day)

I love the balloon I'm holding, it's like the sun breaking through a black sky. The apples on the bed, as I rest, are more symbolic gifts. I felt more than I ever had. Now it was time for sleeping and resting, I needed nothing more.

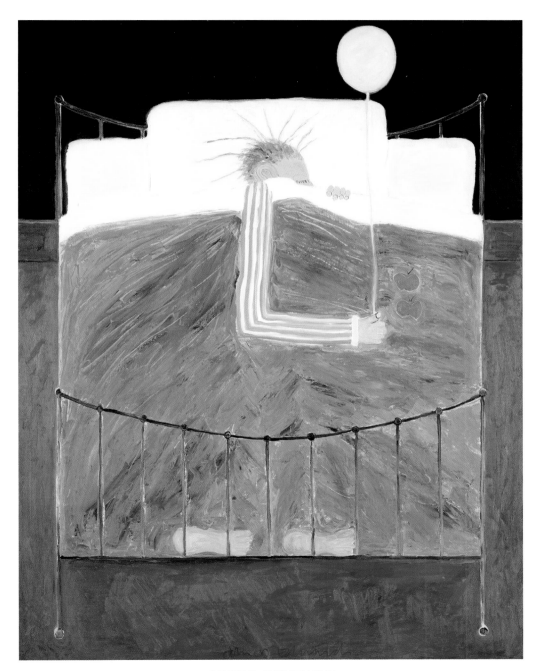

AFTER VISITING

Show Girls

A lot of important art is concerned with big issues. Picasso's Guernica for a start; David Hockney going to paint the Grand Canyon and more recently Damien Hirst's Jesus and the Apostles. All my subjects are close to home, there's a life's work around me and the studio.

The apple paintings developed as a result of changing my diet to lose the weight I had gained through the interferon and chemo. Now there are always apples in the studio. Many such paintings have followed. "Show Girls" came about as I began to find these apples were becoming very sexy.

SHOW GIRLS

Apple Alone

Apple Alone is about being on the edge. There is the sky where there should be the wall. As in several of these apple paintings there is a touch of Magritte, which was a pleasant surprise.

APPLE ALONE

Flemish Apples

In this painting I am getting closer to that "other worldliness" of my experience. The apples are dancing, cancer doesn't like dancing, it prefers depression and despair. So this was good.

The colours and atmosphere reminded me of Northern European painting so I called it Flemish Apples. I really enjoy titling my work; it gives the paintings another dimension and a clue for the spectator.

FLEMISH APPLES

At Home with Jones

Meanwhile life goes on.

A cat painting called "Desert Cat" came back from a collector. It got me thinking about that theme again. Jones was my mother's cat. I had this old painting rolled up so I got it out and finished it eleven years later.

A tribute to those relaxed Sunday family gatherings.

AT HOME WITH JONES

The Welsh Dresser

After so many hospital days it was a pleasure to be home. The chest of drawers seen in "Friends" appears again here, this time with apples. I got the chest of drawers from my sister years ago. It's the one possession that I've kept throughout and it's polished and shining too.

I hope this painting exudes the warmth that this piece of furniture represents to me. The Welsh, in a way, refers to the landscape quality in the painting and my family's connection with it.

THE WELSH DRESSER

Day Out

This teapot has been a feature in my kitchen for years and when I put it with the apples it looked like an Aunt or School Teacher looking over the children, so it became "Day Out".

John D Edwards

DAY OUT

The Mother Bird

Another of my old themes. I began painting this new bird and I wasn't sure where I was going with it. Then sadly my mother, Joan, died. When I returned to the studio before the funeral I realised it was for her, to wish her on her way with love. Also to express my deep gratitude that she had seen me getting well. The colours in the feathers are her colours. Her maiden name was bird so I had the perfect title.

MOTHER BIRD

The Tourist

I'd been coming back from the daily radiotherapy treatments to see a number of birds on bikes on my studio wall. I found this very encouraging. As things improved I painted "The Tourist", a painting about starting out on a new journey. Sometime later I saw that this image represented me leaving the darkness of the cancer on a river like a flowing, golden ray of sunshine.

THE TOURIST

The Dancers (Dancing Brushes)

The apples had started to dance. As I began to sustain longer periods of work, between my increasingly optimistic hospital check ups, my brushes began to dance.

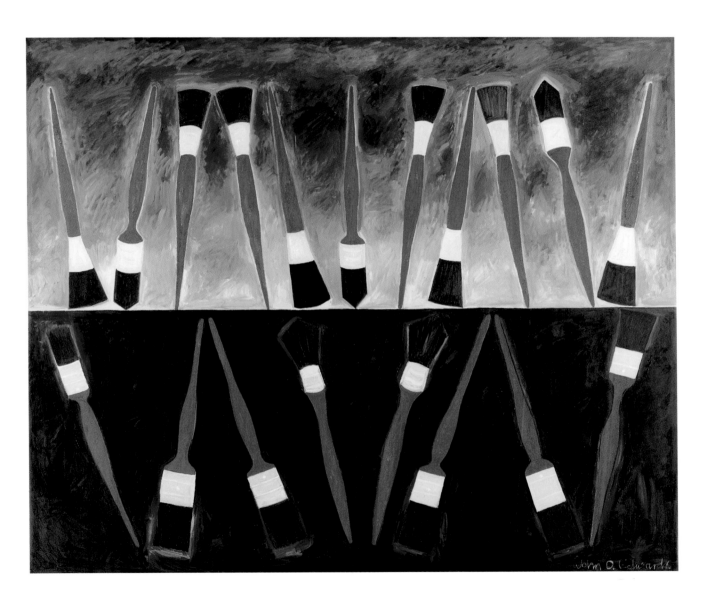

THE DANCERS

Dancing in the Sunlight

The fish from "Friends" were no longer confined to their goldfish bowl; they were now dancing in the sunlight.

DANCING IN THE SUNLIGHT

Sun Soaked Palm

Some say that if they had such a serious or terminal illness they would get out the "things to do before…" list. Before cancer I was always on the go. My illness liberated me from all that. Just to sit and contemplate the stillness of life was now sometimes enough. Just like a cat contemplating an out of reach bird.

SUN SOAKED PALM

Apple Regatta

I was exhilarated when my apples took to the sea.

APPLE REGATTA

Heart in the Sunshine

This is the last painting in this extraordinary story of surviving cancer. I had been taken to some dark places but now I was in the sunshine and my heart was strong.

This is not The End it is just another beginning.

John D Edwards

HEART IN THE SUNSHINE

How Cancer Saved My Life

Getting Through

Cancer still strikes fear in all of us. For so many cancer is associated with 'The End' or at least the beginning of a 'battle' or 'fight for life'. We hear all the time of important people 'losing the battle' or how they 'bravely fought it'. How they 'battled to The End'. Possibilities of cures are discussed often in a way that will enable us to carry on just as before.

On realising that cancer was in my life I began to ask myself how I could change things, how I could help myself? We all have choices in the way we live and how we accept treatment. We can participate and give help to those caring for us.

This has been a journey full of revelations about myself and others, many of whom I would not have had the good fortune to meet but for cancer. I have been to the edge of that dark abyss, I have looked over, climbed in and had a good look around. Having faced every scenario of a life threatening situation I have gently come through having taken responsibility for my health and experienced the freedom of my own mortality. It became clear that the quality of my life was more important than longevity. Apart from all the doctors and nurses offering their help there is so much we can do to help our situation, whatever the prognosis.

John D Edwards

Index,

Tourist Class
72"X82"
Oil On Canvas
1998
Collection of The Artist, London.

Pink Shoes
55"X40"
Paper Mounted On Board
1999
Collection of The Artist, London.

All Will Be Well
38"X51"
Oil On Canvas
1998
Collection of The Artist, London.

Getting Through
45"X43"
Oil On Canvas
1998-1999
Donated By Sharon Spratt Trust To
Teenage Cancer Unit,
Middlesex Hospital, London.

After Visiting, (Easter Day)
48"X36"
Oil On Canvas
1998
Collection of The Artist, London.

Show Girls
36"X48"
Oil On Canvas
1999
Collection, Kate & Colin Birss,
Hertfordshire.

Apple Alone
20"X24"
Oil On Canvas
1999
Private Collection , London.

Flemish Apples
36"X48"
Oil On Canvas
1999
Collection, Mr Grant Denison California.

At Home With Jones
46"X46"
Oil On Canvas
1988-1999
Collection, Mr John Sperling Phoenix
Arizona.

The Welsh Dresser
48"X48"
Oil On Canvas
1999
Private Collection London

Day Out
36"X36"
Oil On Canvas
1999
Collection of The Artist, London.

The Mother Bird
60"X60"
Oil On Canvas
1999
Collection, Charlie & Ruth Middle,
Dorset

The Tourist
60"X60"
Oil On Canvas
Collection, Marion Edwards & Stan
Beanland, Ipswich.

The Dancers, (Dancing Brushes)
70"X80"
Oil On Canvas
1998-2000
Private Collection, Houston Texas.

Dancing In The Sunlight
54"X60"
Oil On Canvas
2000-2001
Private Collection London

Sunsoaked Palm
60"X60"
2000
Oil On Canvas
Private Collection, Cornwall

Apple Regatta
42"X60"
Oil On Canvas
1999
Collection, Mr. Scott Wiltshire

Heart In The Sunshine
70"X66"
Oil On Canvas
2002
Collection of The Artist, London